Contents

T0355275

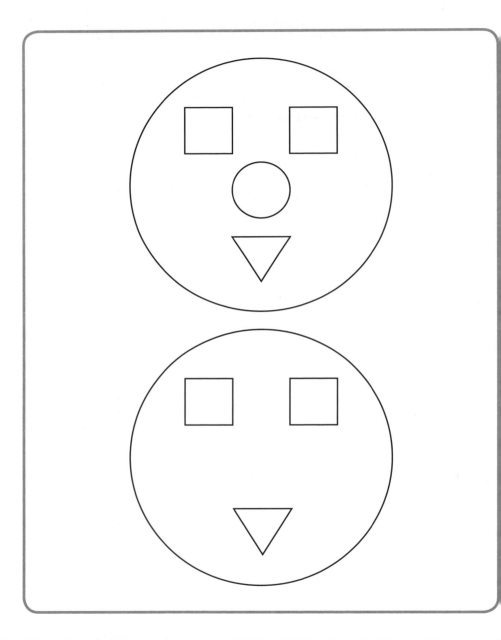

Hello
Recognizing shapes
and patterns

1 Point and say. **2 Draw the missing shapes.** **3 Count the shapes.**

Vocabulary: circle, square, triangle, eyes, nose, mouth, bird, leg, wing

Structures: **What's missing?** (One) (triangle). How many (squares) are there?

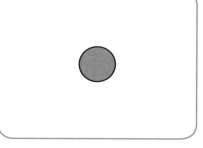

one

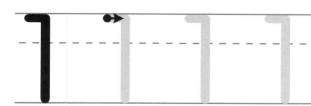

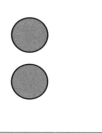

two

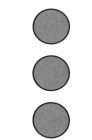

three

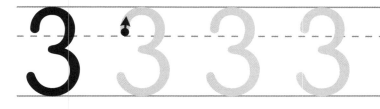

1 Count the dots.　　**2** Trace with your finger and pencil.　　**3** Write the numbers.

Vocabulary:　one, two, three

Structures:　How many dots are there?　(One) dot.

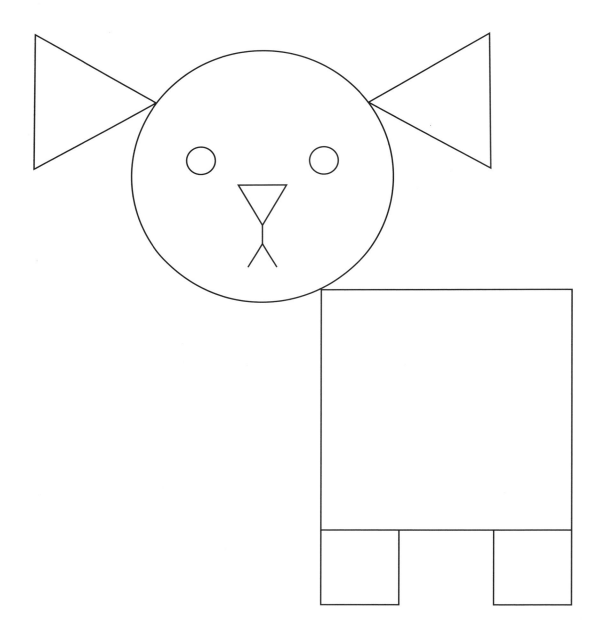

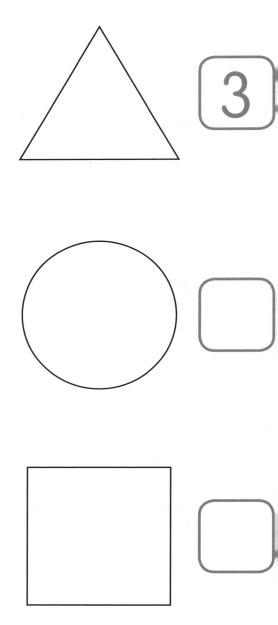

Unit 1
Recognizing and counting shapes

1 Count the shapes and say.   **2 Write the number of the shapes.**   **3 Color the dog.**

Vocabulary: 1–3, dog, Shapes

Structure: This picture uses (3) triangles, (2) circles.

one	two

two	three

three	one
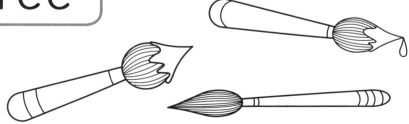	

1 Look and count the objects. **2** Color the correct number of objects. **3** Circle if there are more.

Vocabulary: **more/fewer,** 1–3, bird, birds, flower, flowers, brush, brushes

Structure: (One) (bird), (two) (flowers).

one

~~two~~

~~three~~

one

two

three

one

two

three

one

two

three

Unit 1
Counting objects
in an image

1 Look and count the objects.   **2 Circle the correct number.**   **3 Color if there are three.**

Vocabulary: 1–3, trees, flowers, birds, kites
Structure: How many (trees) are there?

1 Look and point to the first and last object.   **2** Color the first object green.   **3** Choose another color for the last object.

Vocabulary: **first/last**, crayon, eraser, pencil, Colors
Structures: **The first crayon is (green).   The last crayon is (purple).**

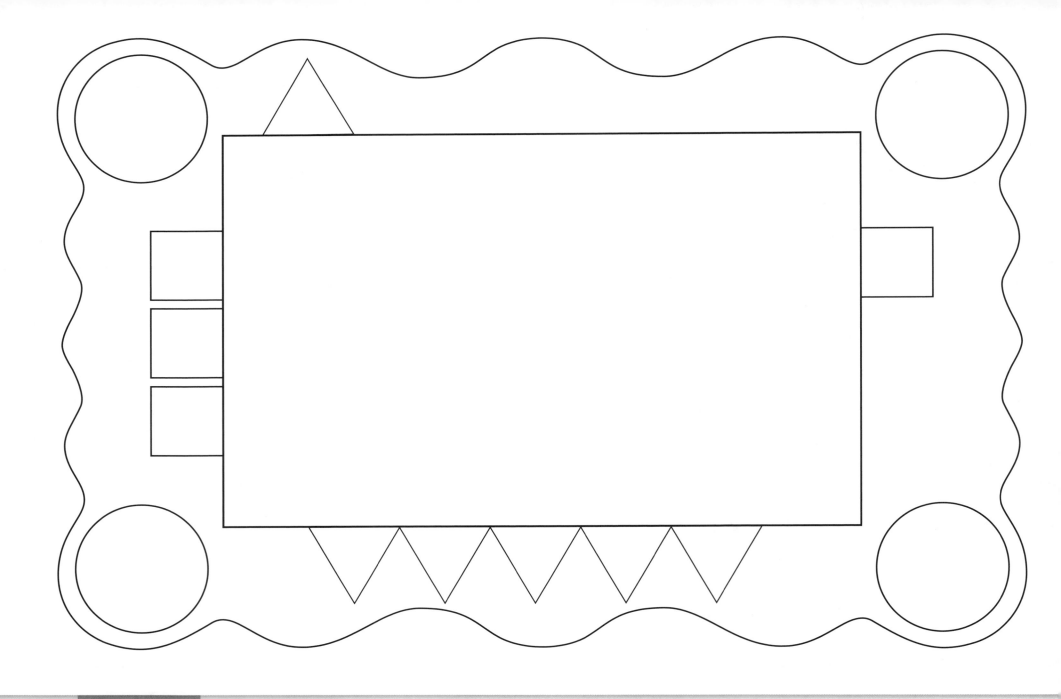

Unit 1
Patterns, shapes
Numbers 1–10

1 Look, say the shapes, and count.   **2 Finish the picture.**   **3 Stick paper shapes to make a picture.**

Vocabulary: 1–10, Shapes, Colors, Art materials

Structures: How many …?   My picture uses (blue) (circles) and …

1 Who's first? Who's last? Point and say.   2 Who's in the middle? Point and say.   3 Color the first child red, the last child brown, and the child in the middle green.

Vocabulary: **in the middle**, first, last, Anna, Sam, May

Structures: **He's in the middle.**   She's first.   She's last.

Unit 2

Following sequences 1–10

Shapes

1 Follow the numbers with your finger and pencil. **2 Count the shapes.** **3 Color the shapes.**

Vocabulary: 1–10, monkey bars, slide, swing, circle, rectangle, triangle, park

Structures: Do you see (the circle)? How many (triangles) can you see? One (circle), two (triangles).

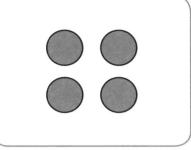

four

4 4 4 4 4

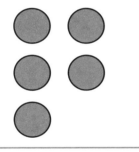

five

5 5 5 5 5

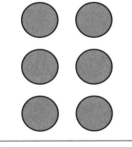

six

6 6 6 6 6

1 Count the dots.　2 Trace with your finger and pencil.　3 Write the numbers.

Vocabulary:　four, five, six

Structure:　How many dots are there?

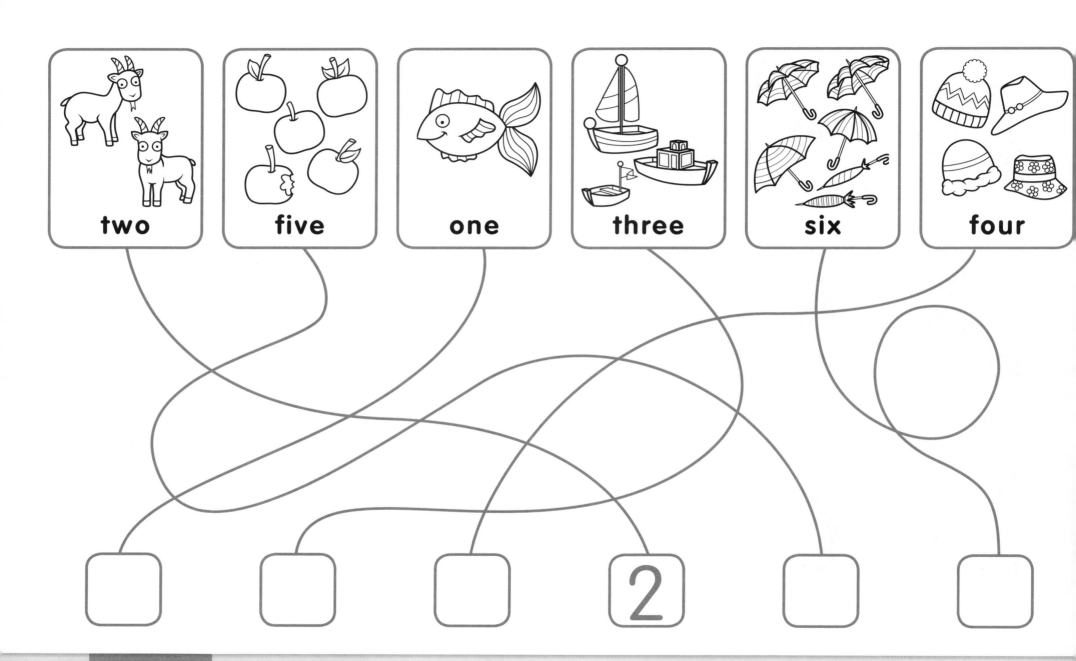

two five one three six four

2

Unit 2
Counting 1–6,
one–six

1 Count the objects.   **2 Follow and write the number.**
Vocabulary: one fish, two goats, three boats, four hats, five apples, six umbrellas
Structure: How many (goats) are there?

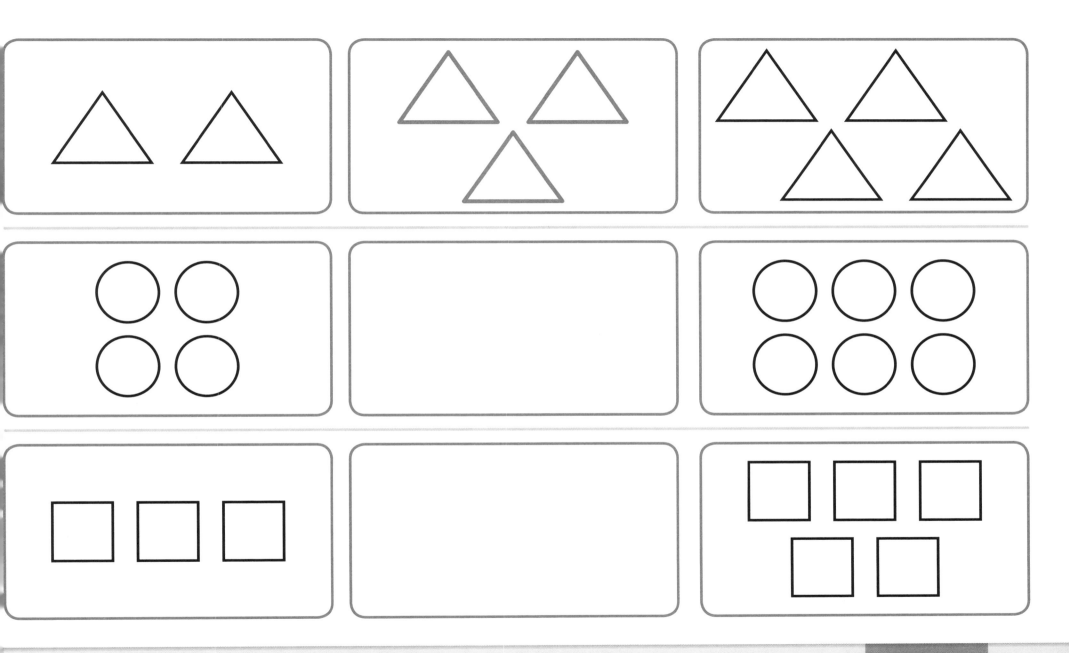

1 Count the shapes. **2** Draw the correct number of shapes in the middle. **3** Color if there are six.

Vocabulary: 1–6, in the middle, Shapes

Structure: How many (triangles) are in the middle?

Unit 2
Counting to 6
One more

1 Count the children. Count the balls.   **2 How many balls are missing?**   **3 Draw the missing ball.**
Vocabulary: **one more**, 1–6, child, ball
Structure: How many more balls do we need?

1 How many boys are in the picture? How many children are there?   **2** How many girls are in the picture? How many children are there?   **3** Look and match the same.

Vocabulary: boy, girl, children, **same/different**

Structures: How many (boys) are there?   **This is the same/different.**

Unit 3
Counting to 6
Estimation, addition

1 Count the dolphins.   **2 Where are there more dolphins? Color.**   **3 Draw more dolphins to make 6 in each picture.**

Vocabulary: 1–6, dolphins, more/fewer, the same

Structure: Where are there more dolphins?

seven

eight

1 Color and count the dots. 2 Trace with your finger and pencil. 3 Write the numbers.

Vocabulary: seven, eight

Structure: How many dots are there?

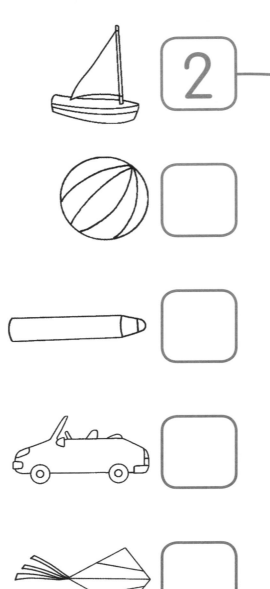

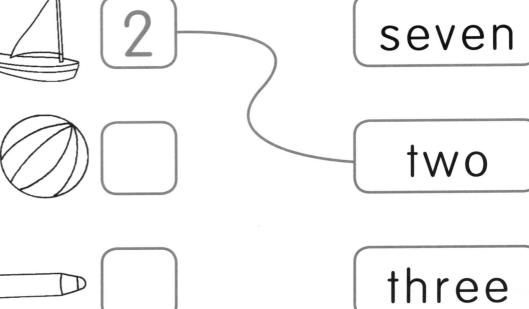

2

seven

two

three

eight

five

Unit 3
Revision 1–8,
one–eight

1 **Count and write.**   2 **Match the numbers.**   3 **Color if there are eight.**
Vocabulary: one–eight, Toys
Structure: How many (boats) are there?

five

eight

four

two

1 Look.   2 Count the candles.   3 Draw the missing candles.

Vocabulary: two–eight candles, birthday, cake, fewer, more

Structures: How old is (he/she)?   There are fewer candles.   How many are missing?

Unit 3
Tall/short
Taller/shorter

1 Who's tall? Circle. **2** Who's short? Color. **3** Draw someone tall and someone short in the family.

Vocabulary: **tall, short, taller, shorter,** May, Sam, Anna, mom, dad

Structures: **Who's tall/taller? Who's short/shorter?**

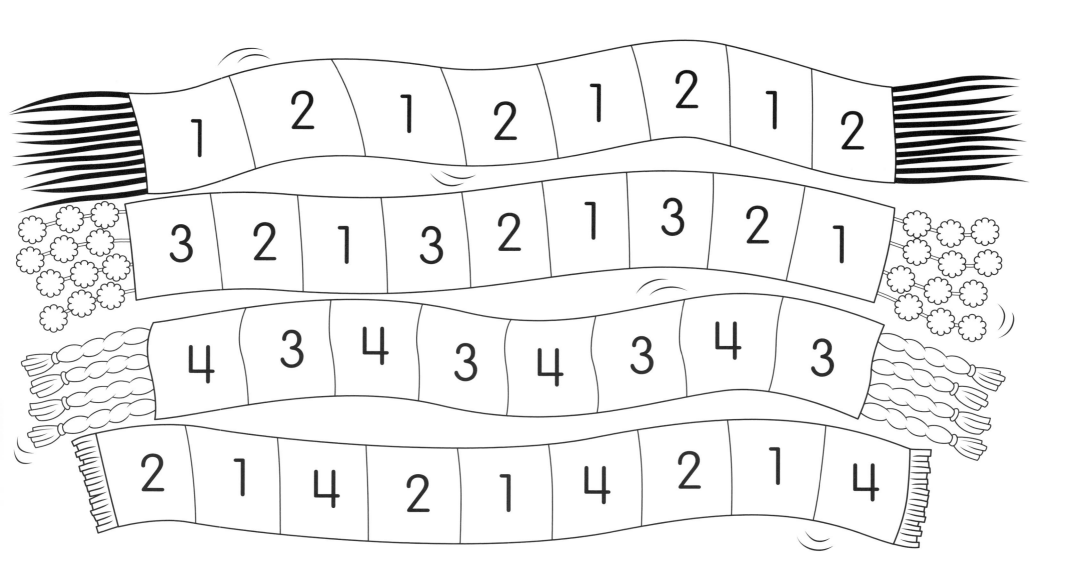

1 Color 1, 2, 3, 4 with four colors. Make patterns.   2 Circle your favorite pattern.

Vocabulary: 1–4, pattern, Colors

Structure: **What's your favorite pattern?**

Sunday	2
Monday	6
Tuesday	1
Wednesday	4
Thursday	7
Friday	3
Saturday	5

Unit 4
Sequencing 1–7

1 Look and say.   2 Match.   3 What's the first day of the week? What's the last day of the week?
Vocabulary: 1–7, first/last, Days of the week
Structure: What's the first/last day of the week?

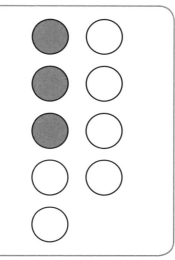

nine

9 9 9 9

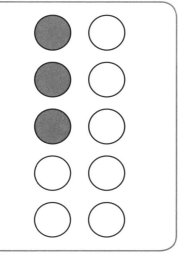

ten

10 10 10 10

1 Color and count the dots.   2 Trace with your finger and pencil.   3 Write the numbers.

Vocabulary: nine, ten

Structure: How many dots are there?

Unit 4
Counting 9, 10
Number formation

23

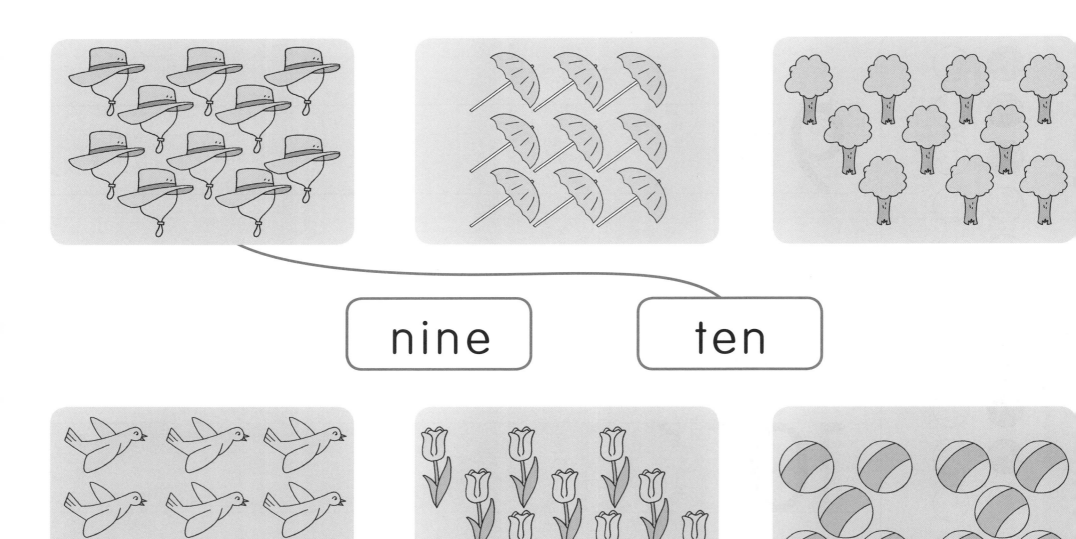

nine

ten

Unit 4
More than

1 Look and count. **2 Match.** **3 Circle if there are more than 9.**

Vocabulary: **more than**, 9–10, hats, umbrellas, trees, birds, flowers, balls
Structure: Circle if there are more than (9).

1 **How does he feel? Say.**   2 **Follow with your finger and pencil.**   3 **How does he feel now?**

Vocabulary: cold, wet, warm, dry, boots

Structures: How does he feel?   He's (cold).

Unit 4
Addition to 9

1 Find the differences.   **2 How many are missing? Count and write.**   **3 Draw the missing things.**

Vocabulary: 1–9, hats, flowers, trees

Structure: How many are missing?

1 **Look and count.** 2 **Write the number.** 3 **Where's the teddy bear in the kitchen/bedroom? Circle and say.**

Vocabulary: 1–8, teddy bear, car, pencil, ball, book, sofa, cupboard, bed, bath, floor, door, kitchen, living room, bedroom, bathroom, on, in, next to, above

Structures: Where's the (teddy bear) in the (bedroom)? It's (on) the (bed).

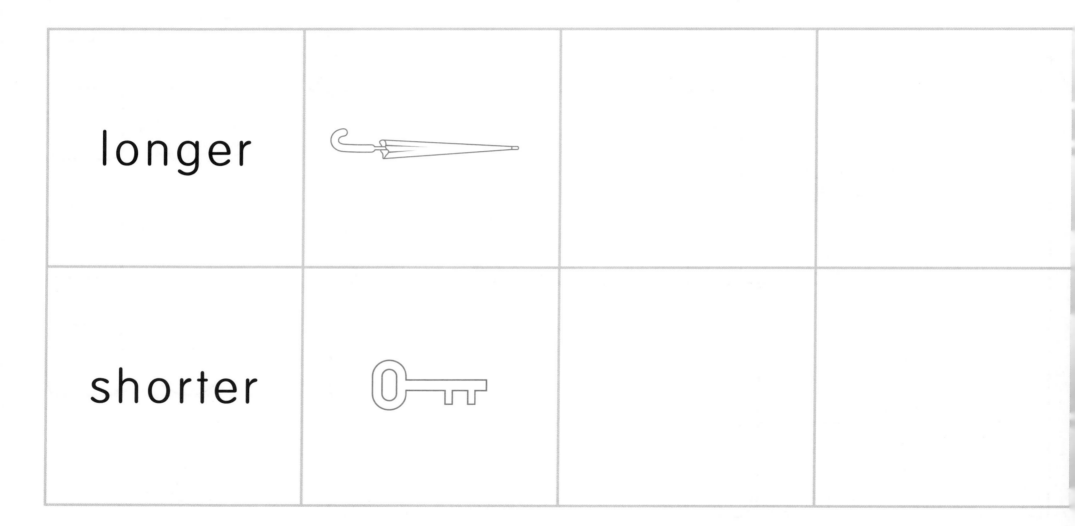

longer			
shorter			

Unit 5
Comparing length

1 Look at the pencil.　　**2** Find and draw something longer.　　**3** Find and draw something shorter.

Vocabulary:　longer, shorter, umbrella, key

Structures:　The (umbrella) is longer than the pencil.　　The (key) is shorter than the pencil.

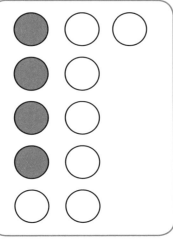

eleven

11 11 11 11 11

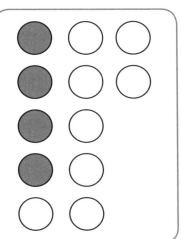

twelve

12 12 12 12

1 Color and count. 2 Trace with your finger and pencil. 3 Write the numbers.

Vocabulary: eleven, twelve

Structure: How many dots are there?

12 eleven ⟨twelve⟩

eleven twelve

eleven twelve

eleven twelve

Unit 5
Counting to 12
Addition

1 Count, write, and circle. **2 Color if there are twelve.** **3 Draw one more if there are eleven.**

Vocabulary: eleven, twelve, chairs, ducks, tables, dolls, one more

Structure: How many (dolls) are there?

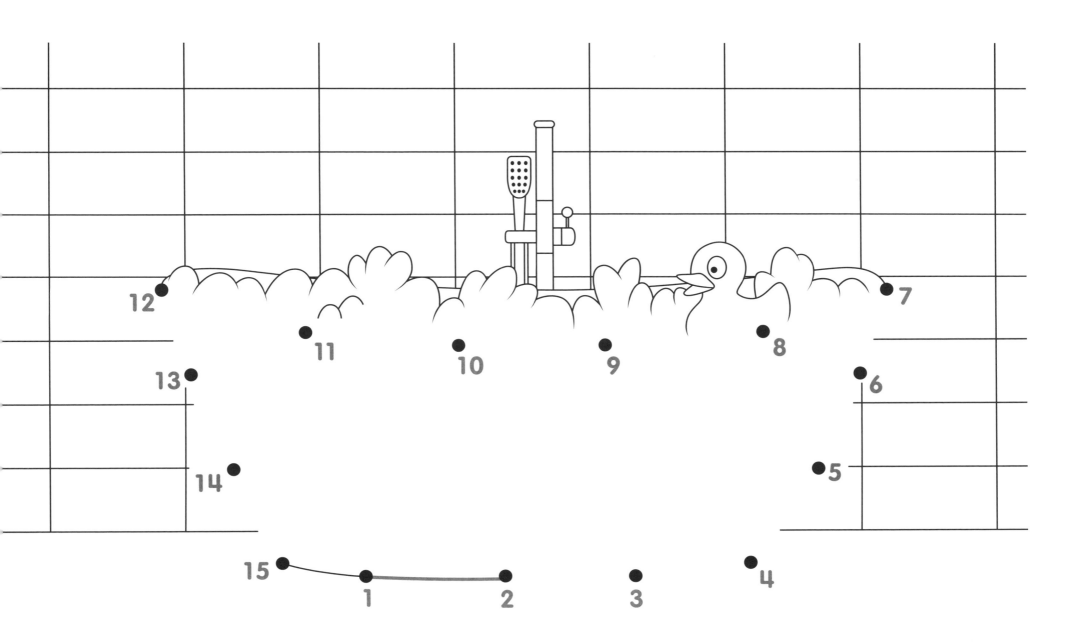

1 Say the numbers. **2 Connect the dots with your finger and pencil.**

Vocabulary: 1–15, bath, bathroom

Structures: What is it? It's a …

Unit 5
Addition to 12

1 Count the toys on the shelves.   **2 Write the number.**   **3 How many boats/cars are there altogether?**

Vocabulary: eleven, twelve, boats, cars, shelf, cupboard

Structure: **How many (boats) are there altogether?**

ok

1 **Look and say.**   2 **What's next?**   3 **Match.**

Vocabulary: **cucumber**, apple, carrot, strawberry, grapes
Structures: **What's next?** (Cucumber).

Unit 6
Comparing number of items

1 Which hive has more bees?   **2** Count and circle.   **3** Say.

Vocabulary: hive, bees, more/fewer, first, last, middle
Structures: Which hive has more bees?   How many bees live in the first/last hive?

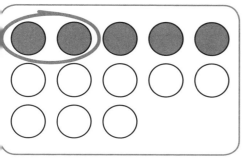

thirteen

13 13 13 13

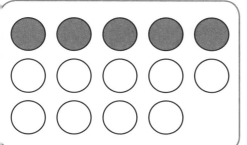

fourteen

14 14 14 14

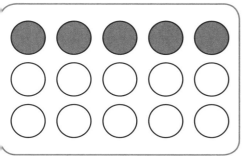

fifteen

15 15 15 15

1 Color and count the dots.   **2** Trace with your finger and pencil.   **3** Circle the dots in twos. Write the numbers.

Vocabulary: thirteen, fourteen, fifteen

Structures: How many dots are there?   Circle the dots in twos.

Unit 6
Counting 13, 14, 15
Number formation

35

five

thirteen

fourteen

ten

10

six

twelve

fourteen

nine

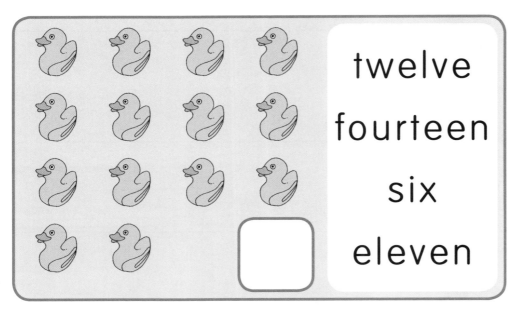

twelve

fourteen

six

eleven

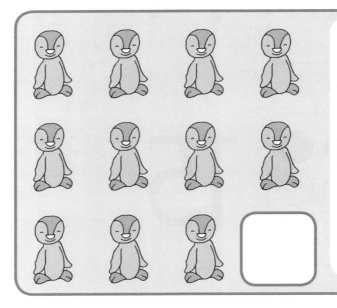

thirteen

ten

eleven

four

Unit 6
Counting to 14
Skip counting by 2

1 **Count and write.**   2 **Circle the number.**   3 **Circle in twos.**

Vocabulary: 1–14, teddy bears, fish, ducks, penguins

Structures: How many (teddy bears) are there?   Circle the (teddy bears) in twos.

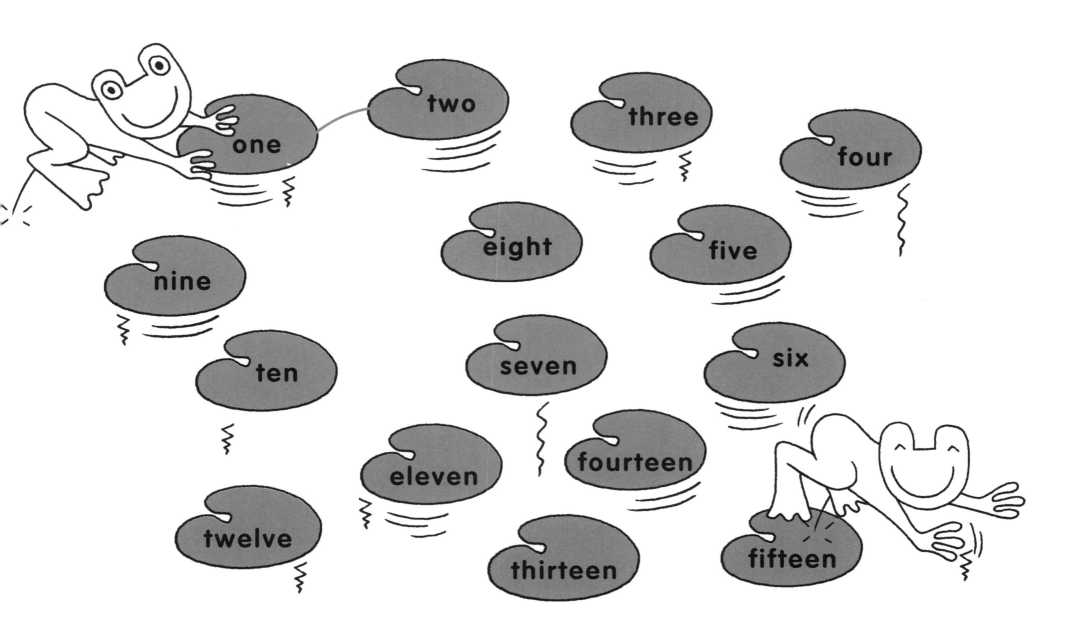

1 Follow the number words with your finger.　2 Say the numbers.　3 Follow the number words with your pencil.

Vocabulary:　one–fifteen
Structures:　What's next?　(Two, three ...)

Unit 6
Sequencing number
words one–fifteen

37

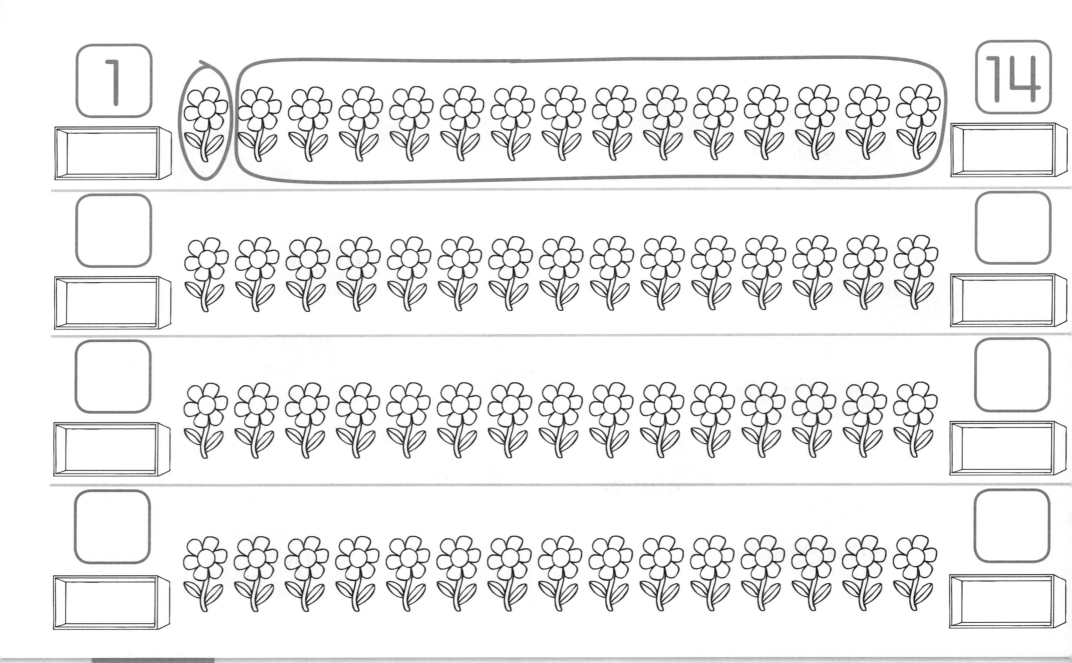

Unit 6 Addition to 15

1 Put a different number of flowers in each basket. 2 Circle the flowers. 3 Write the number of flowers in the box.

Vocabulary: 1–15, basket

Structure: How many flowers are there in this basket?

1 Find and circle 5 differences.   **2 Close your book and remember.**   **3 How many are missing?**

Vocabulary: flowers, trees, more, fewer, Farm animals

Structures: How many (ducks) are missing?   There are …   There are more/fewer here.

The farmers have 15 brown chickens and 1 white chicken.

The farmers have 16 brown cows and 1 black and white cow.

Unit 7
Counting
Addition

1 Count and say. **2 Read.** **3 Color.**
Vocabulary: 1–17, farmers, chickens, cows
Structures: How many (cows) do the farmers have?   They have (16) (brown) (cows).

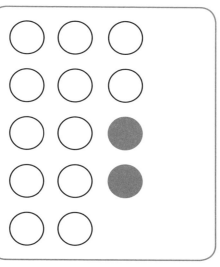

sixteen

16 16 16 16

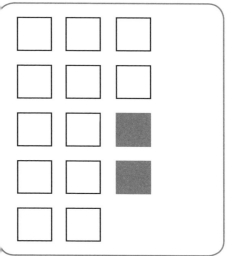

seventeen

17 17 17 17

1 **Count and draw.**   2 **Trace with your finger and pencil.**   3 **Circle the dots and squares in twos.**

Vocabulary: **sixteen, seventeen,** dots, squares

Structures: How many (squares) are there?   How many are missing?   Circle in twos.

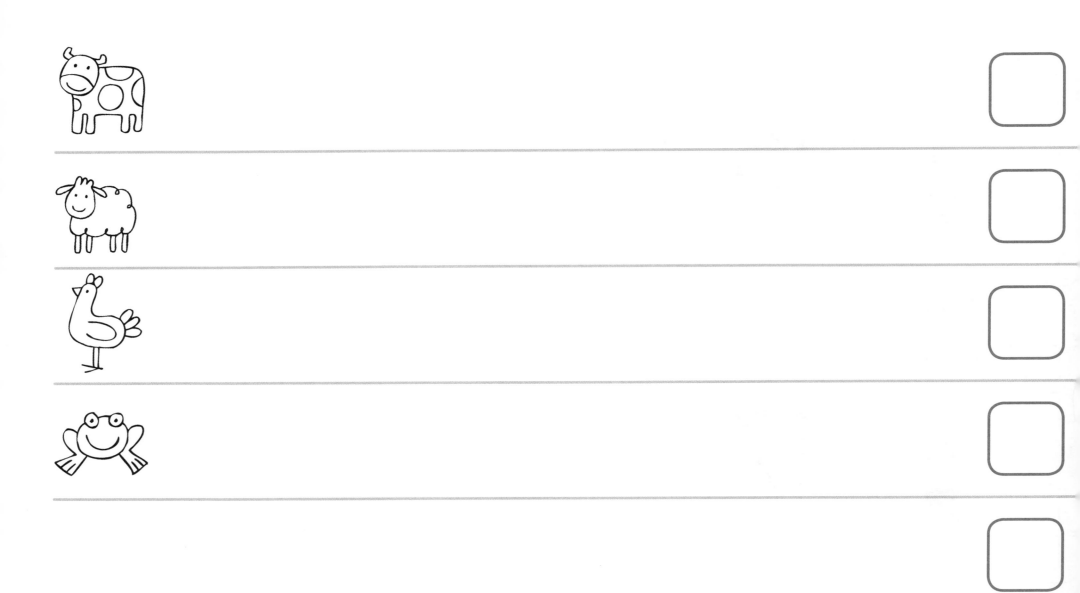

Unit 7
Addition

1 Draw one more animal in each line than in the previous line.　**2** Draw your favorite animal in the last line.　**3** Count and write.

Vocabulary:　cows, sheep, chickens, frogs

Structure:　Draw one more (sheep).

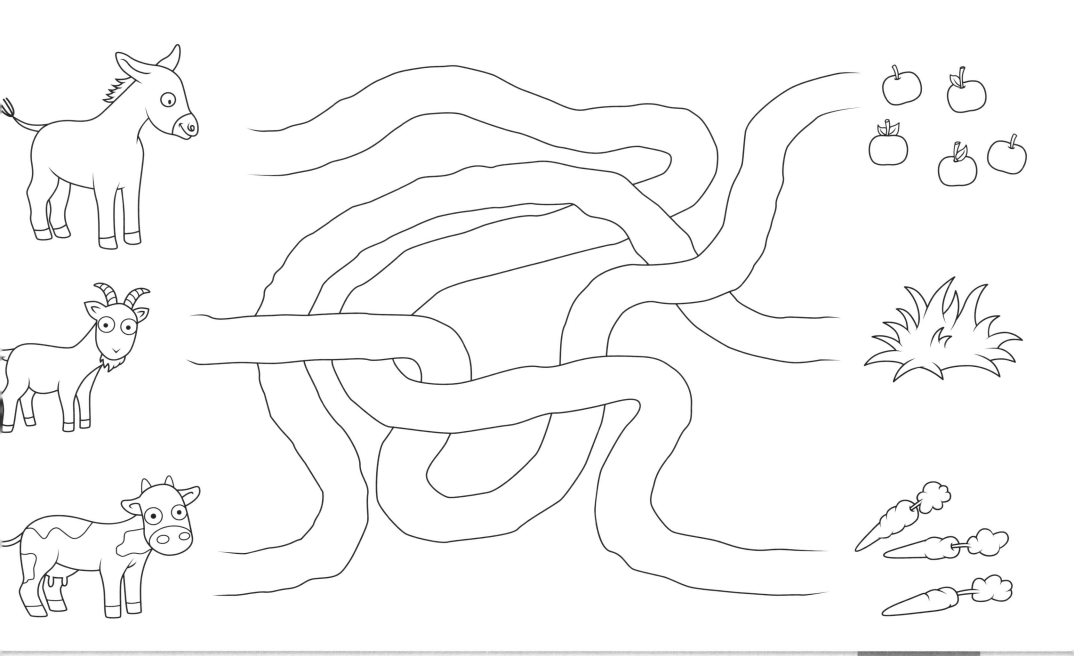

1 Follow with your finger and pencil.   2 What does the donkey eat?

Vocabulary: donkey, goat, cow, carrots, apples, grass
Structures: What does the (donkey) eat?   It eats (carrots).

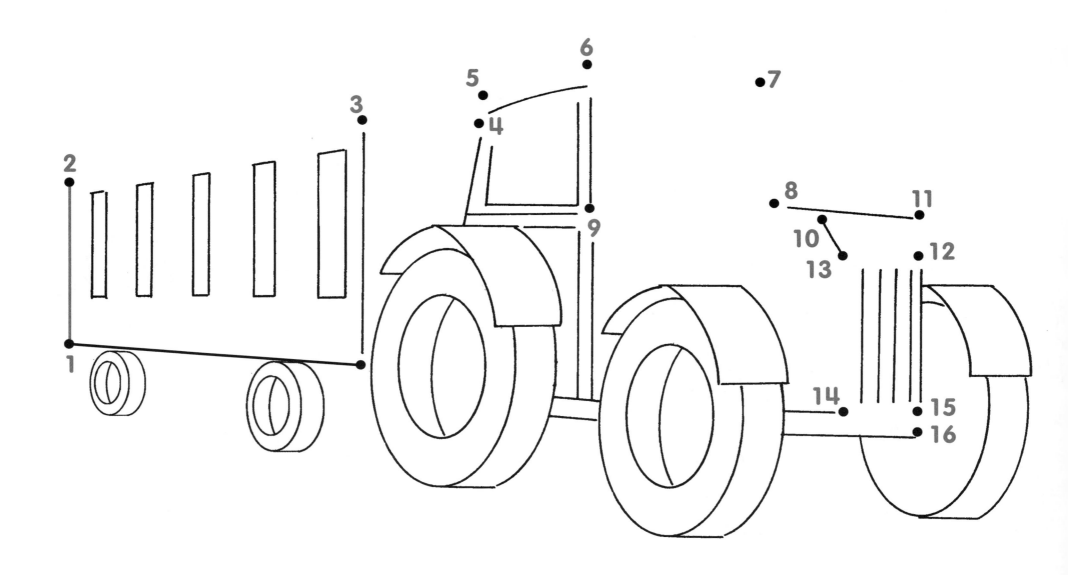

Unit 7
Sequencing 1–16

1 Connect the dots with your finger and pencil. What's on the farm? **2 Color.**

Vocabulary: 1–16, truck
Structures: What's on the farm? A ...

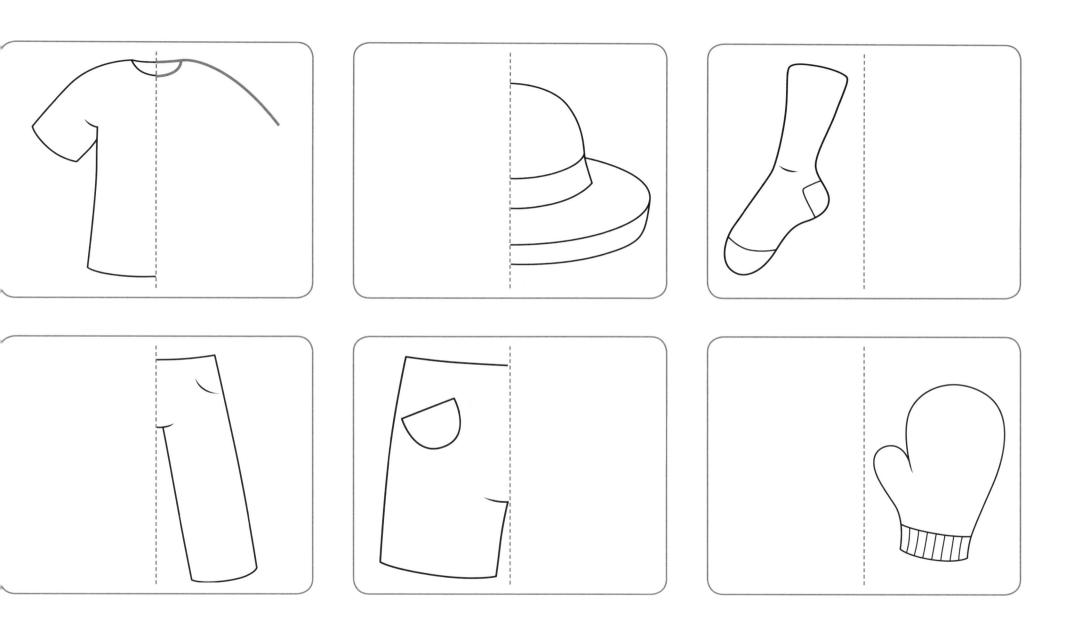

1 **What is it? Point and say.**   2 **Complete.**   3 **Color if there is a pair.**

Vocabulary: **a pair**, T-shirt, hat, socks, pants, shorts, mittens

Structure: Is it a pair?

Unit 8
Identifying similar patterns

1 Find and color the matching socks.   2 How many socks are there?   3 How many pairs are there?

Vocabulary: ten, twenty, socks, pairs
Structure: How many pairs are there?

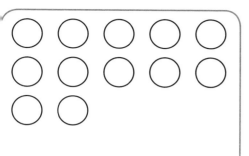

eighteen

18 18 18 18 18

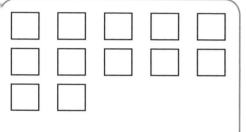

nineteen

19 19 19 19 19

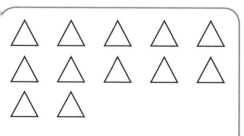

twenty

20 20 20 20

1 Count and draw.   2 Trace with your finger and pencil.   3 Circle the dots, squares, and triangles in twos.

Vocabulary: **eighteen, nineteen, twenty**, dots, squares, triangles
Structures: How many dots are there?   How many are missing? Circle in twos.

Unit 8
Numbers 18, 19, 20
Skip counting by 2

47

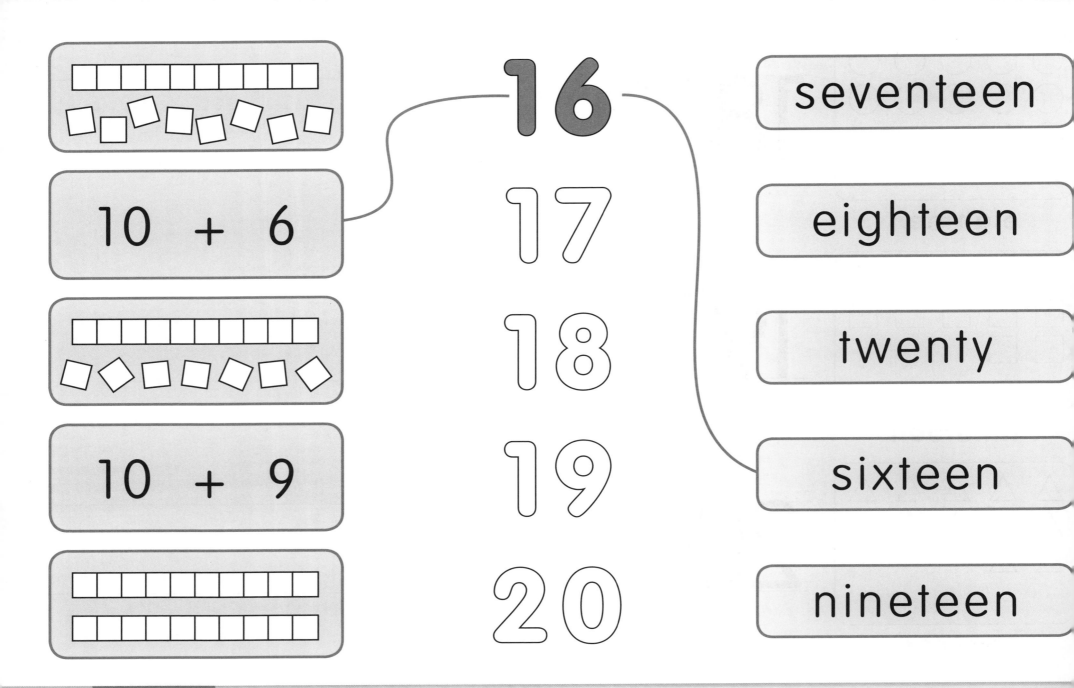

Unit 8
Addition 10 +

1 Count and match.   2 Color the numbers.   3 Say.

Vocabulary: 16–20
Structure: Ten and (six) make (sixteen).

twelve

fifteen

twenty

eleven

seventeen

nineteen

1 Write the missing numbers.   2 Match.   3 Color the T-shirts.
Vocabulary: eleven–twenty, 11–20
Structures: What's missing?   Twelve …

Unit 8
Sequencing 11–20   49

Unit 8
Measuring using
non-standard units

1 Measure the T-shirts. Write.　　2 Measure the boy's body.　　3 Color the T-shirt that fits the boy.

Vocabulary:　1–4, big/**bigger**, small/**smaller**, the same size

Structure:　How big is this T-shirt?

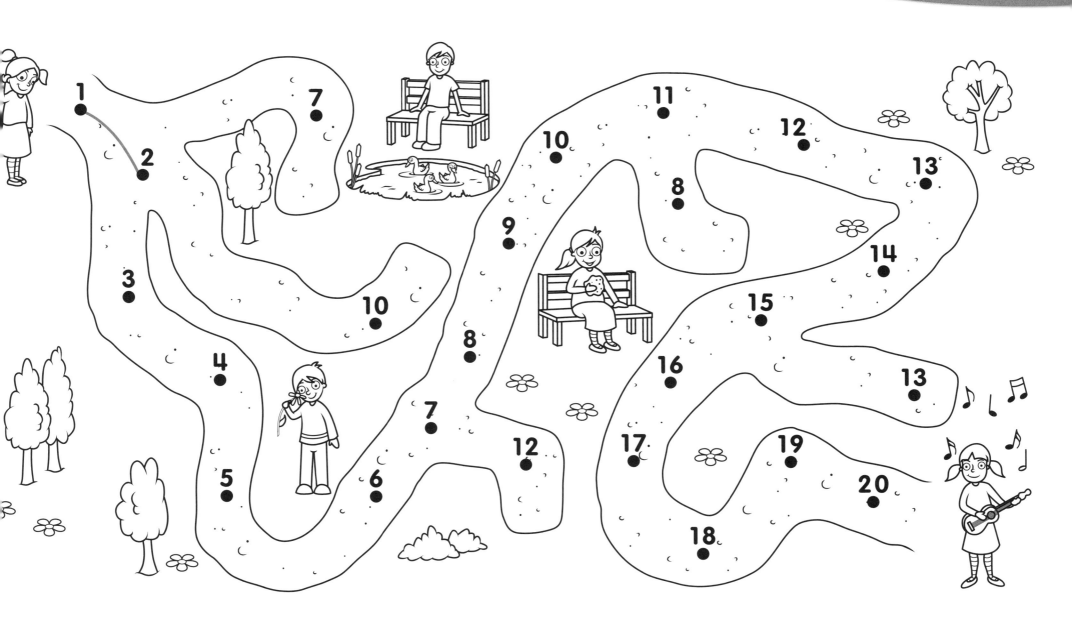

1 **Follow the numbers with your finger and pencil.**   2 **Who's quiet? Color.**

Vocabulary: 1–20, girl, boy

Structures: What's next?   Who's quiet?

Unit 9
Spatial awareness

1 Draw a bee above every flower.   **2** Draw a ball next to the girl.   **3** Draw a boy behind the tree.

Vocabulary: bees, ball, tree, flowers, girl, mom, dad, next to/above/behind
Structure: Draw (a ball) next to (the girl).

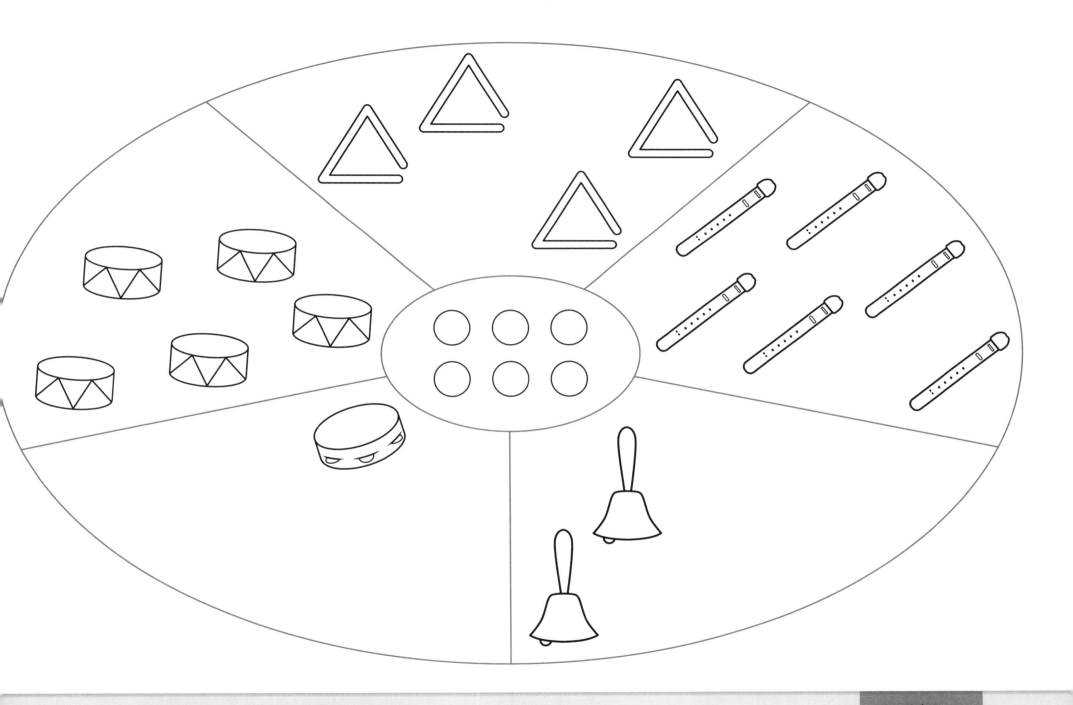

1 Count the dots.   2 Draw the same number of instruments.   3 Color the loud instruments.

Vocabulary: tambourines, triangles, drums, bells, recorders, loud, quiet

Structures: How many are there?   How many are missing?   Is (the drum) quiet?

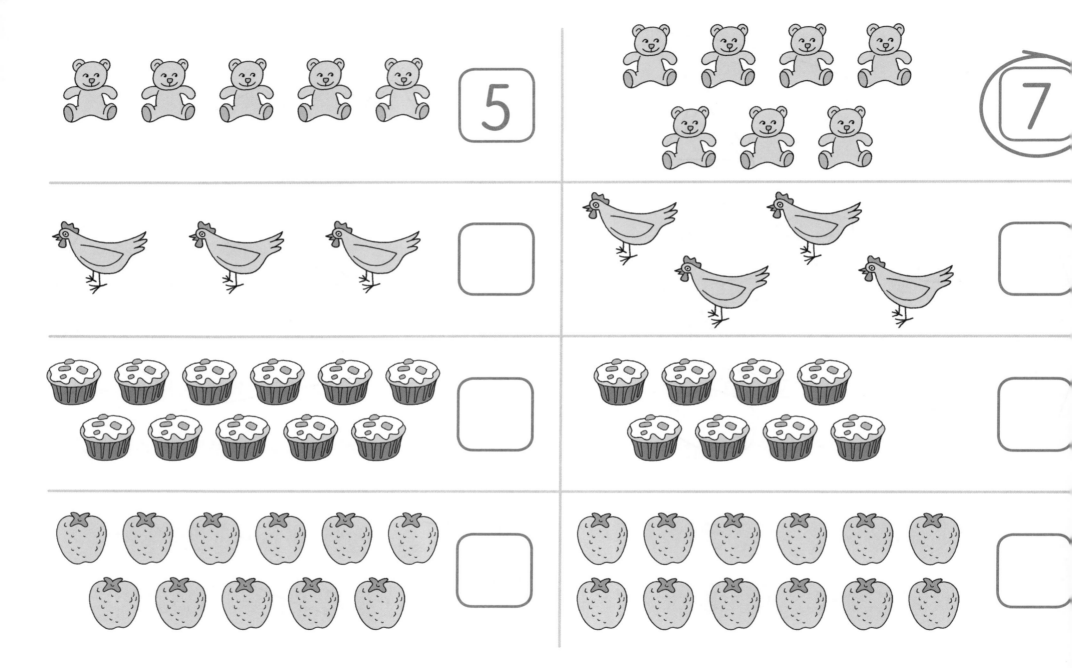

Unit 9
Comparing sets,
bigger/smaller

1 Count and write.   **2 Which number is bigger?**   **3 Circle.**

Vocabulary: 1–20, teddy bears, ducks, cakes, oranges, bigger/smaller

Structures: How many (teddy bears) are there?   **Which number is bigger?**